Nancy Faber

Colorful solos which develop

musical expression and creativity at the piano

CONTENTS

Rainbow Splendor

Con moto (♩=116-126)

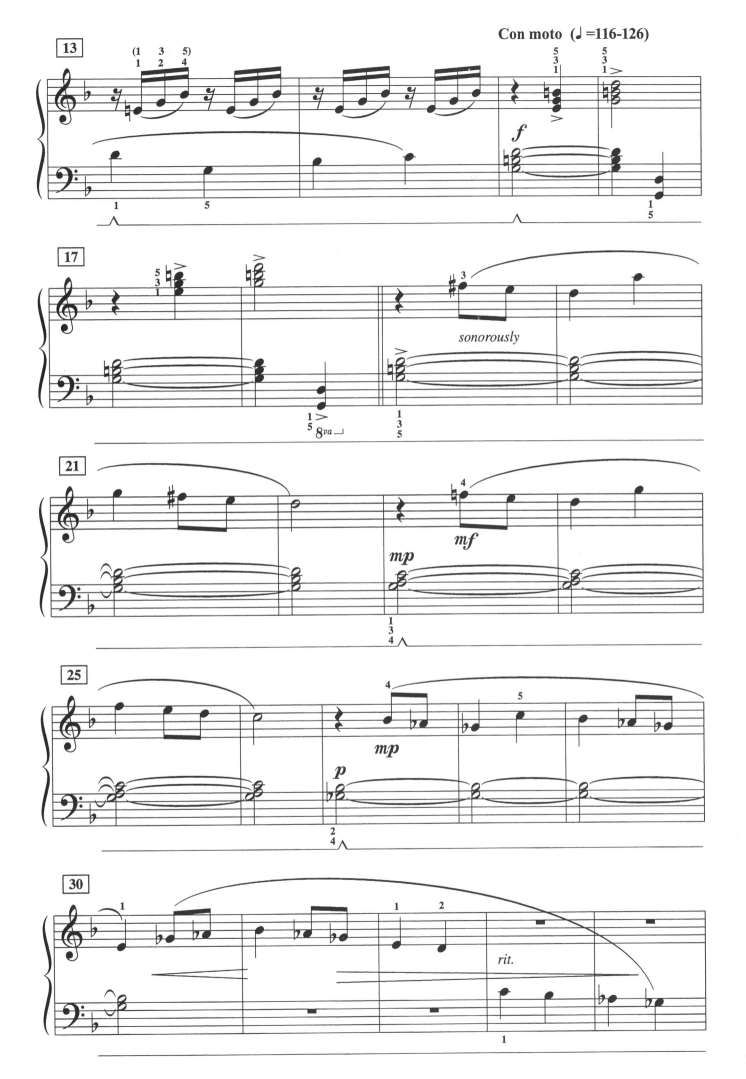

4

To Have a Rainbow

Lyric by Jennifer MacLean

rain and sun must work to - geth - er   to   cast this mag - ic

poco rit.

a tempo

spell.

p   *f*   R.H. over

mp   *mf*   L.H. over

When you're feel - ing   sor - ry,

mp   *mf*   *mp*   or

when you're feel - ing   *melody*   blue;

mf   *p*

Shimmering Waterfalls

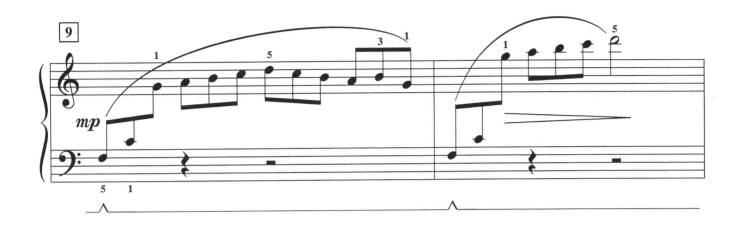

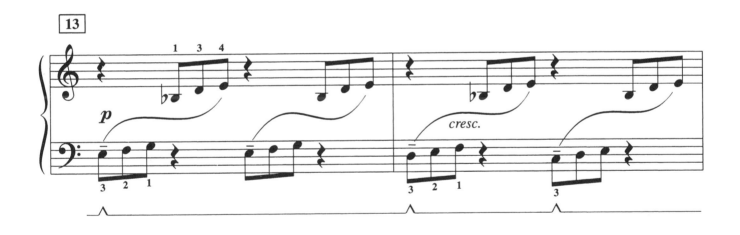

BOTH HANDS

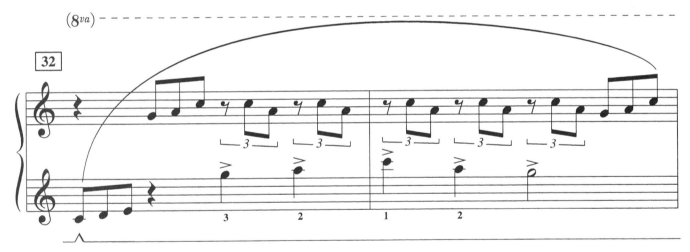

Valse Indigo

Allegro moderato, espressivo (♩ = 120-152)

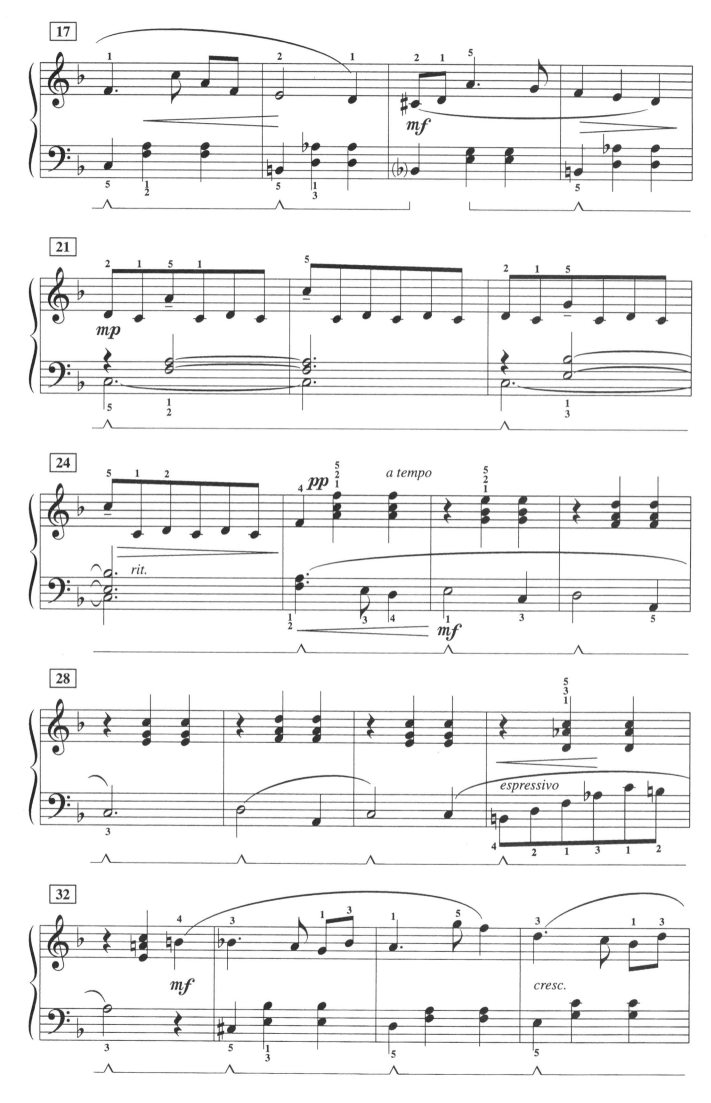

Crystalline Rag

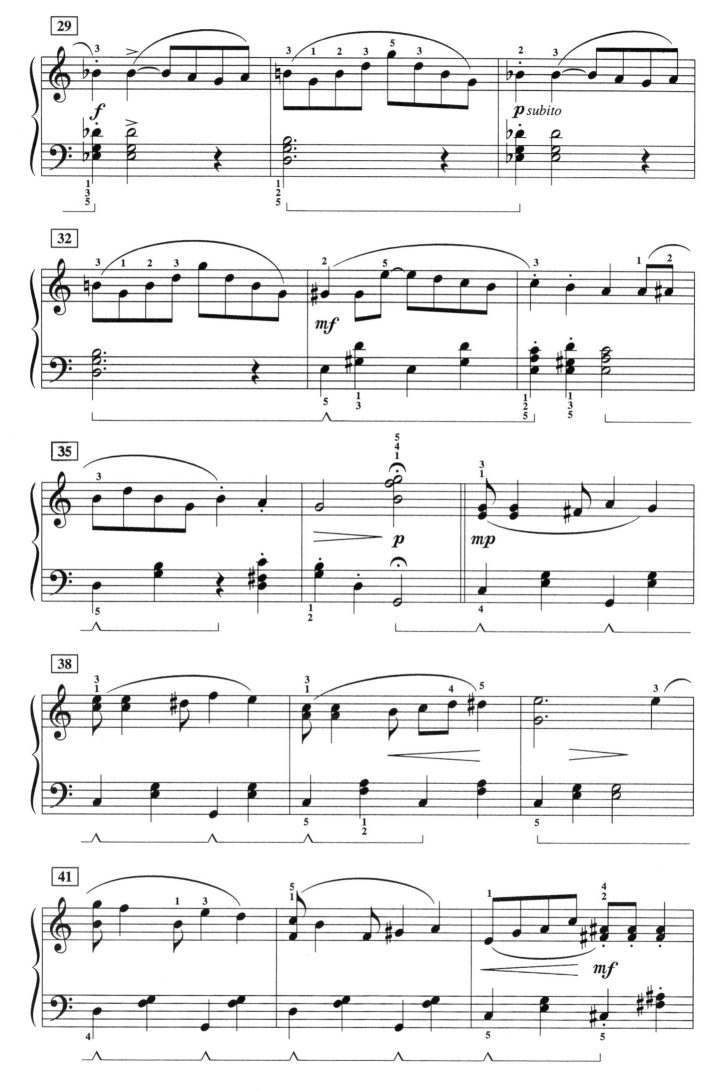

Amber Rhapsody

Flowing, "in two" with rubato ($\.= 54\text{-}60$)

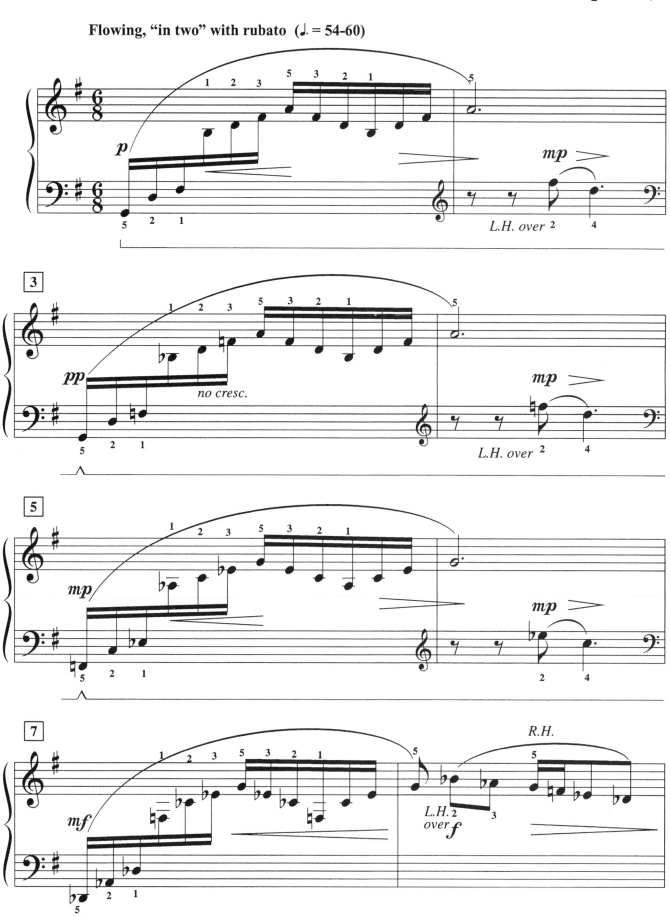

22

FF1105

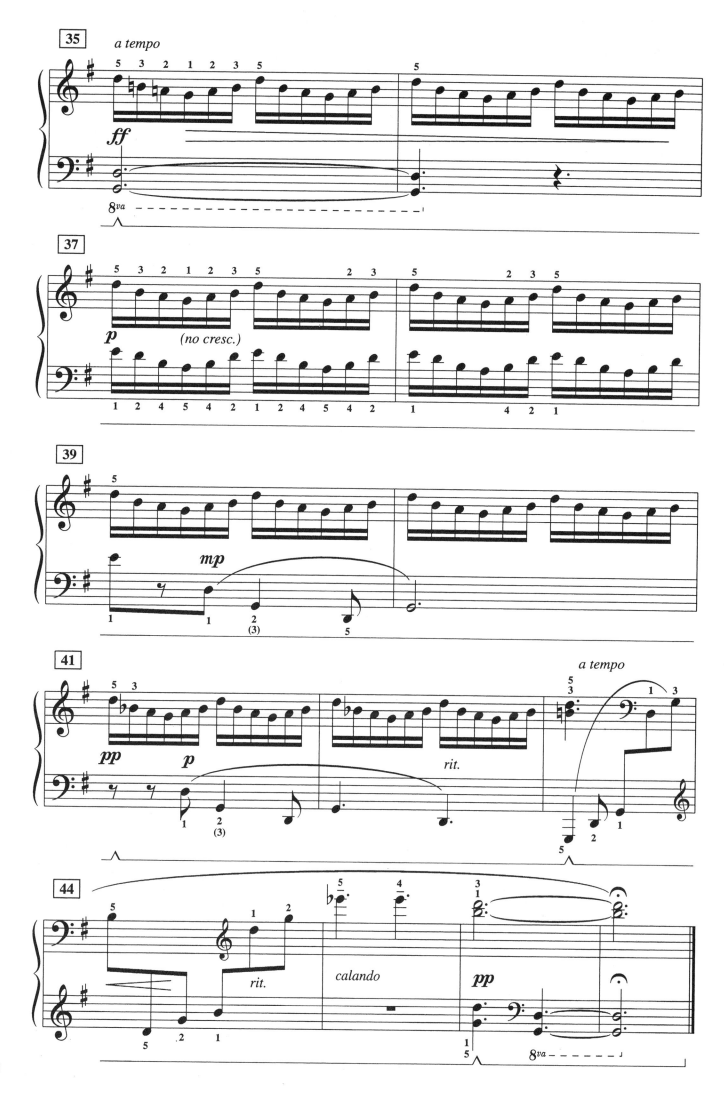